Alphabet Trucks

Samantha R. Vamos

Illustrated by **Ryan O'Rourke**

A B C D E F G H I J K L M N O P Q R S T U V W X Y Z

ini **Charlesbridge**

Start the engines.
Lift and load.
Shift the gears and
hit the road.

Vroom! Rumble! Zoom!

Alphabet trucks.

A is for apple truck,
carting produce to the store.

B is for box truck,
with a rolling rear door.

C is for cargo truck,
shipping goods across land.

D is for dump truck,
moving gravel, dirt, and sand.

E is for elevator truck.
Raise the forklift—up it goes!

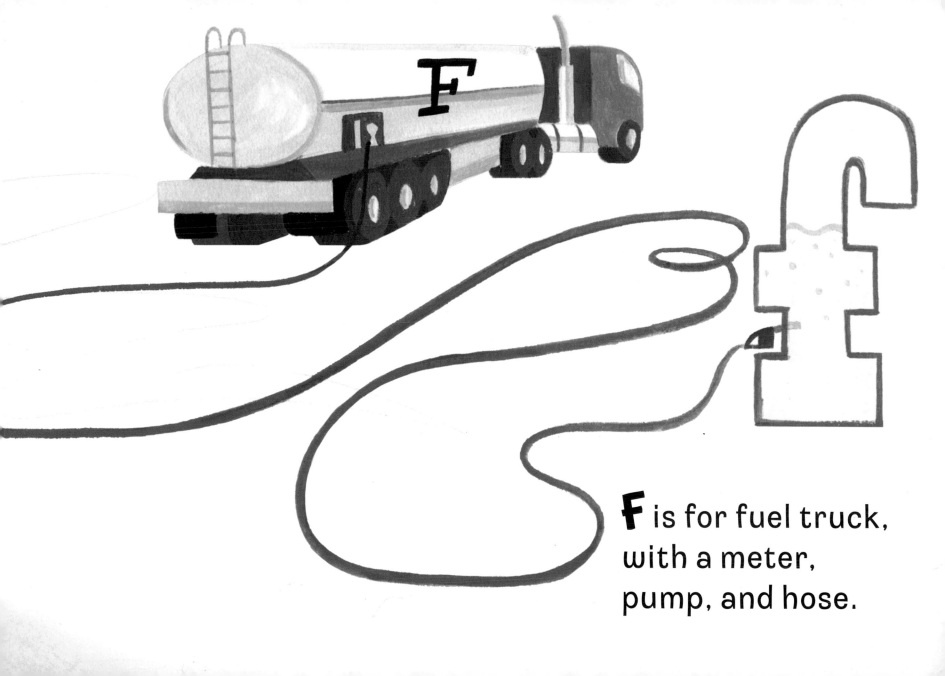

F is for fuel truck,
with a meter,
pump, and hose.

G is for grapple truck,
and its grabby, massive claw.

H is for horse truck,
full of water, feed, and straw.

I is for ice-cream truck,
with frozen treats to taste.

J is for junk truck,
removing scrap and waste.

K is for knuckle-boom truck.
Its rear crane folds up tight.

L is for lowboy truck,
with its drop in deck height.

M is for mixer truck,
for stirring concrete.

N is for news truck, reporting from the street.

O is for ore truck,
carrying tons
in weight.

P is for pickup truck,
with a bed and tailgate.

Q is for quint truck: hose, tank, ladders, and pump.

R is for recycle truck—
less trash to fill the dump.

S is for snowplow truck—
snowy streets to clear
and groom.

T is for tow truck,
with a hook, chain, and boom.

U is for U-Haul truck.
New homes and
friends to greet.

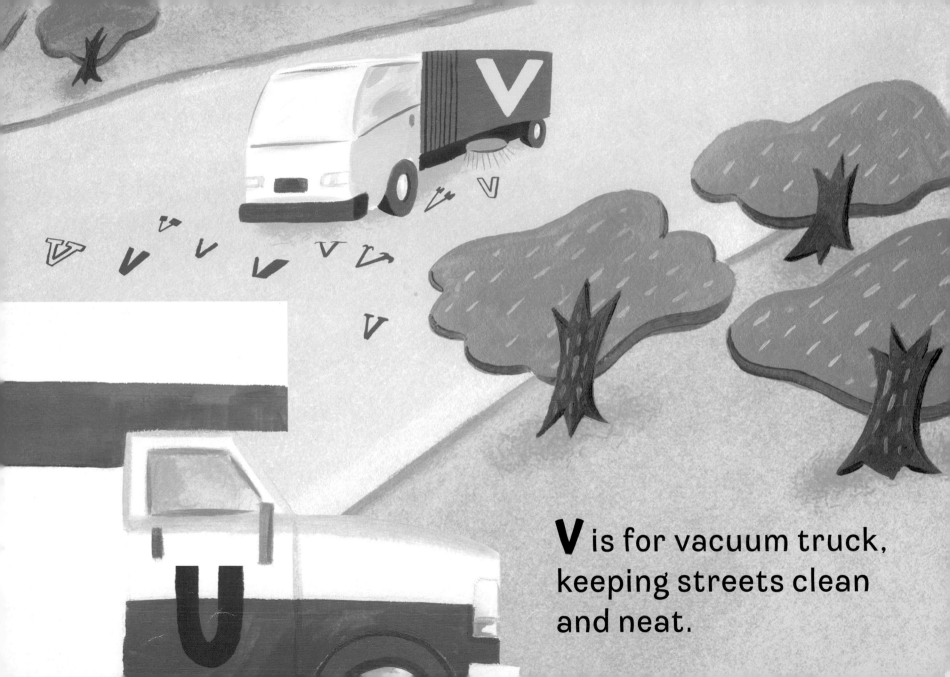

V is for vacuum truck, keeping streets clean and neat.

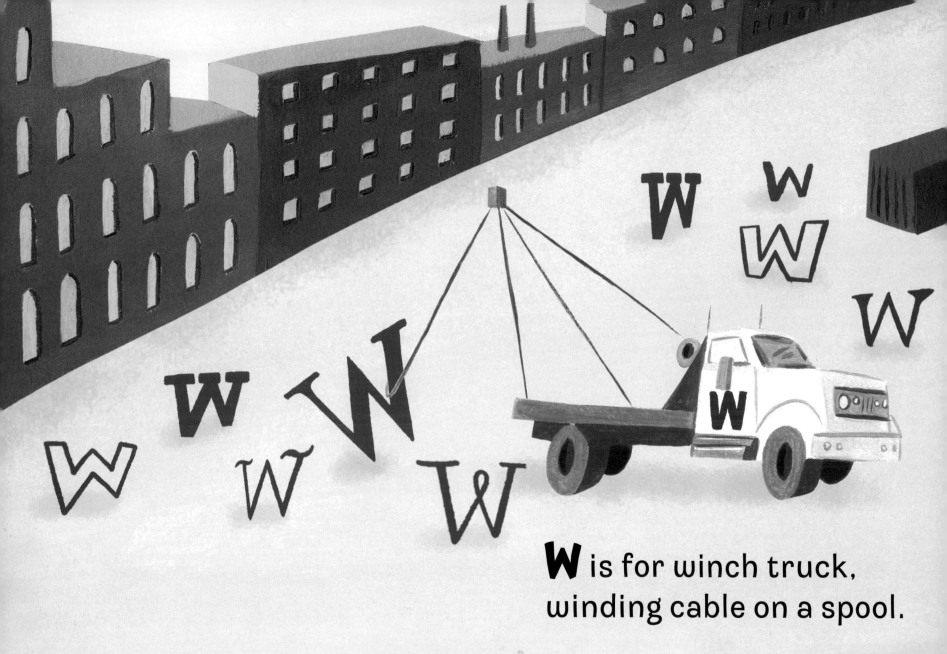

W is for winch truck,
winding cable on a spool.

X is for X-ray truck,
scanning contents with a tool.

y is for yard truck,
slowly moving as it hauls.

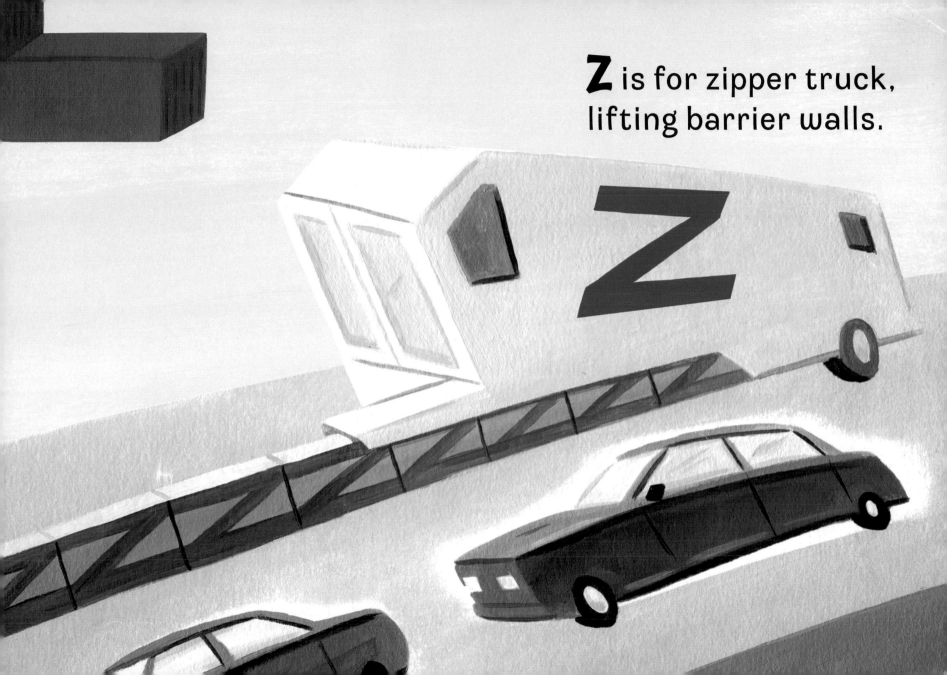

Z is for zipper truck,
lifting barrier walls.

Day and night,
just watch and see.
Trucks work hard
from A to Z.

Published by Charlesbridge
85 Main Street
Watertown, MA 02472
(617) 926-0329
www.charlesbridge.com

Library of Congress Cataloging-in-Publication Data
Vamos, Samantha R.
  Alphabet trucks / Samantha R. Vamos; Illustrated by Ryan O'Rourke.
    p. cm.
  Summary: In simple rhyming text, this book follows hardworking
trucks from A to Z.
  ISBN 978-1-58089-428-9 (reinforced for library use)
  ISBN 978-1-60734-918-1 (ebook)
  ISBN 978-1-60734-600-5 (ebook pdf)
1. Trucks—Juvenile fiction. 2. Alphabet books—Juvenile fiction.
[1. Trucks—Fiction. 2. Alphabet—Fiction. 3. Stories in rhyme.]
I. O'Rourke, Ryan, ill. II. Title.

PZ8.3.V32537Alp 2013
[E]—dc23   2012024404

Printed in China
(hc) 10 9 8 7 6 5 4

Illustrations done in oil and acrylic on illustration board
Display type set in Chaloops by Chank Co.
Text type set in Jesterday by Tjarda Koster—Jelloween
Color separations by KHL Chroma Graphics, Singapore
Printed by Jade Productions in Heyuan, Guangdong, China
Production supervision by Brian G. Walker
Designed by Diane M. Earley

For Greg and Jackson:
G is for Gratitude. L is for Love. A is for Always.
In memory of Robin Whitlock Smith:
B is for Brave, Beautiful, Beloved.
—S. R. V.

F is for Family. Huge thanks to my family
for helping Trish and me with all the changes
we've been through in the past year.
—R. O.